JN440346

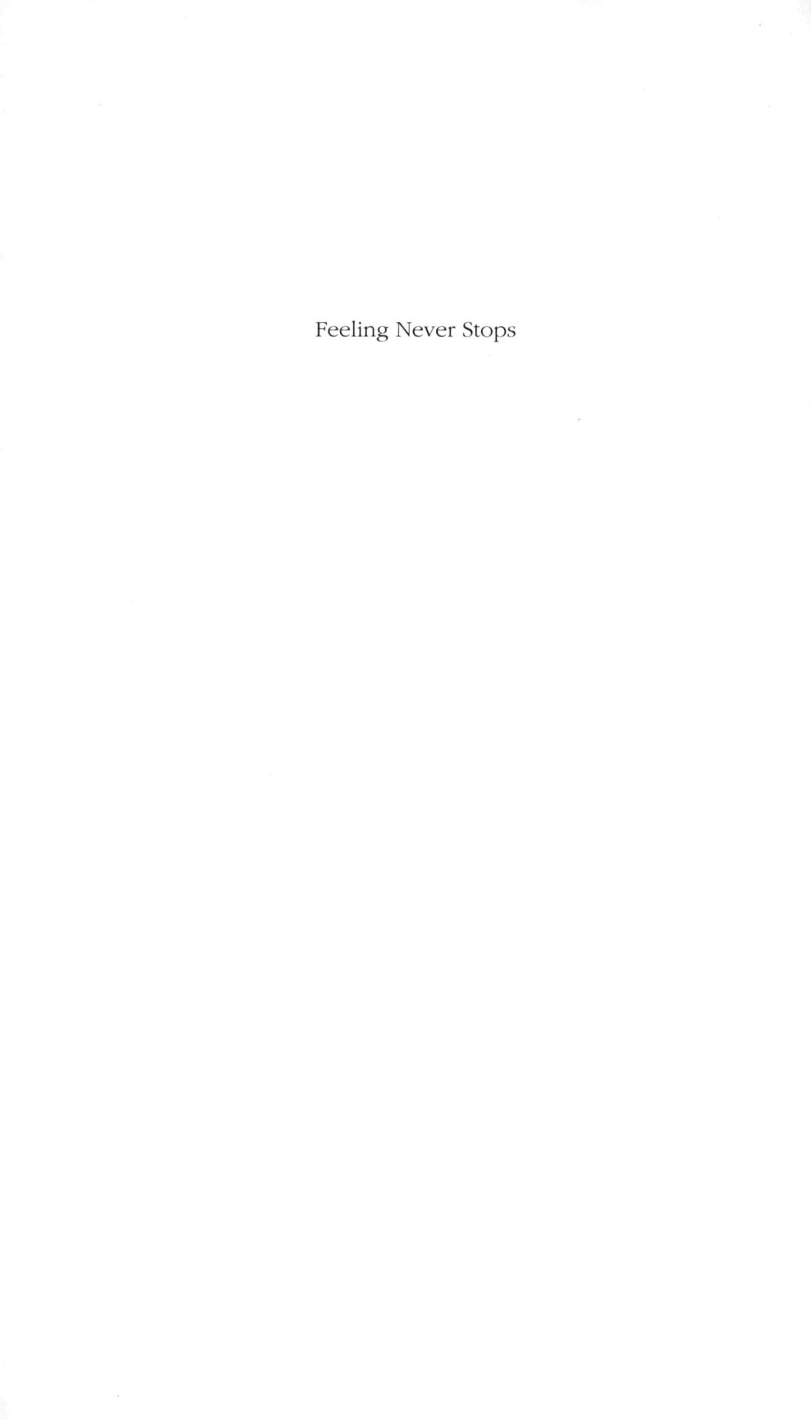

Feeling Never Stops

Feeling Never Stops

A collection of new poems by Ahn Joo-cheol
Translated by Brother Anthony of Taizé

Contents

FEELING NEVER STOPS

Someone with an Open Back

One night

I was looking at the back of a person
climbing up a steeply sloping sidewalk.

One night

I really did see someone with an open back.

This world's hole was there
and I couldn't look away.

Darkness was entering
through that back.

I could not count
but once the darkness had filled that back,
a deeper darkness came pouring
from the back.

I saw a man with an open back.

Someone with an open back was climbing
a sloping path.

Turning Off the Light and Lying Down

From time to time a car passes.
The moon shines down; it was small yesterday
and today it's slightly smaller.

Size doesn't matter to a shining moon.

In order for darkness to accumulate and become darkness
a little more darkness has to pile up
but now I have enough darkness.

Returning back along the path I had taken
I braced my knees as I reflected that

all the thoughts I have ever had are fragments composing me.

Isn't fear regarding life when you don't know where it will stop
in some ways the joy of enduring this life?

I cannot get to sleep
because I live with the things I fear
or maybe because I secretly enjoy them.

After turning off the light and lying down, when I look out the window,

I can see people walking into the empty darkness outside the window.

The thought that I too am there
in the darkness like an inner pocket is warm, but
is it wider inside the darkness or outside the darkness?

Compared to the moonlight shining today,
it doesn't matter very much.

The moonlight is probably froth, too.

As the Sun Sets Strand by Strand

As gentle waves draw the sunset out of the water strand by strand

As a child learning to ride a bicycle pedals into time that will never return

As a small, neat shoulder leans on a big, hard shoulder

As a small shoulder swells as soon as it leans, becoming bigger and harder than a big shoulder

As a pet dog wagging its tail and barking turns

into a lion and runs along the river bank, pulling its owner along

As a yacht turns and turns when the wind cuts corners

As an early evening moon watches the waves at sunset

As if looking down pale, amazed like at first sight

As photographers press the shutter towards the sun with its eyes all blurred

As the hard, red sun caught on the roof of the apartment

can't control its heavy head

As a pack of darkness accumulates in a shattered place

Informal Sorrow

If you are not accurately sad, you will shed tears unreasonably.

You need informal sorrow.

Informal sorrow that is very small
and has not yet become the past

Can become a joy
and not become tears

can become a sorrow
and not become tears.

By one single mistake I come closer to myself.

When by one single mistake I have a feeling that the end is not far off

maybe it means another beginning is ready.

When you can no longer approach bad dreams,

When you can no longer avoid the fear that bounces you around,

You need an informal sorrow that has not become sorrow.

Don't wait

Until you can't pick anything up,

until you can protect yourself in the worst way,

You need informal sadness that survives.

Miracles are regrettable, and luck that has not run out is problematic, but

Just as great faith and great secrets help each other most,

you need the informal grief

that does not become sorrow,

does not form an edge for tears.

Walking Beside the River 1

I walk beside the river.

Since I still have strength

At a loss what to do with that remaining strength

I walk on, roughly honing from the outside
the anger that begins to take shape following the riverside.

Until I'm worn out and drowsy
Until I'm worn out and able to go to work tomorrow

Until I can't deal with my boss at work because I'm so weak

I walk beside the river.

Still I have the strength
to lose weight

In order to grow even a few grams happier with that remaining strength
In order to endure this life even just a few grams lighter

Before anger arises,
before regret arises,

In order to use the remaining strength, I walk beside the river

Taking the dog,
having gone out taking the dog dragging myself along hard

Since strength remains,
in order to waste the remaining strength

Roughly

I walk beside the river

Clouds That Have Vanished

When I roll my eyes following flying dragonflies,
the dragonflies seem about to lay eggs in my eyes.

Why doesn't fatigue accumulate, no matter how urgently
I pursue the sky released by the dragonflies?

Am I asking them to lay eggs in my eyes?

If a death blooms in my eyes and does not fade,
next to the leaves trembling finely in the wind

I'll shake.

I'll shake, flipping over,

I'll shake, tumbling down

If I shake even when I'm dead, every time I shake

it will be just like when I was alive.

Bored?

No.

Shabby?

Even if you flip over a question like that, it's boring

Clouds that couldn't produce rain

float on, soaking the wings of the dragonflies with pale shadows.

Dragonflies fly under the clouds that float on and disappear,
no telling how many times they shake before they disappear.

No matter how I roll my eyes following the dragonflies,
the clouds that have vanished do not return.

The Completed Snack Bar

A child crawls until it arrives at another child.
An old man dies and arrives at his final age.

A death certificate is a name like
a dead person standing up and digging his own
grave.

A dead person is a name like
digging a grave with a living person until the sun
sets.

Digging without knowing whose grave it is,
the mind inclines

Flowers bloom and arrive at flowers,
and as flowers fall, they once make flowers complete.

The snack bar kid puts off homework until there are no more customers,
the snack bar kid starts dictation when there are no more customers,

The snack bar kid approaches perfection while dictating,
dumpling soup when the dumplings are cooked and float,

noodles when they approach the broth that enables them to recall memories,

chairs when they are repeatedly filled with hips.

They approach completion, but are not complete.

The snack bar kid who has finished dictation is about to be completed.

The customer who selects his menu is complete.

The kid's mother is completed as she adds the noodles.

The kid is about to arrive at a new kid.

When most incomplete,

when all are each one,

when those moments all overlap

The snack bar wriggles.

It is trying to complete a snack bar that no one knows about.

Feeling Never Stops

One who sheds tears for a dead person is a family member, even if they're not part of the family. There is no need to perfect doubt like cutting meat delicately.

Even if the last name the dying old man called was not that of the person holding the old man, the difficult mystery surrounding the name is something nobody knows.

The sound of age growing in all directions from the place where the old man's age stopped is audible.

It's difficult to grant the request of someone dying, and it's difficult not to grant it.

The way gunfire goes off in distant mountains and doesn't stop until the gunfire subsides is the fact that we have to stay longer in this world.

Just as the person who left and the person who came back is different, just as we grow farther away, the more we try to become the same.

If the remotest place in the world is the place where I'm sitting right now, I have nothing to say to you. Because I was tired of hunting the past and tired of the sorrow that goes smoothly.

Is it because I lack many worries that I worry a little?

The person who left saying he was going to live fell off the roof, came back and has already died, and is dying again.

Did your consolation cross over to the old man?

Why don't unconfirmed feelings stop?

Let's Start Worrying

Right, let's start worrying.

Shall I worry while it rains and until it stops? Shall I start worrying before it rains? I wish the answer could come into a place where everything is blocked. Luckily. Because that is a wish that cannot be fulfilled. Because I don't need to go to help myself. Of course, it doesn't mean that the road leading me to me is not a long one. If I could reach myself after walking a long way, it would be raining heavily there. I think it's better to worry first. If we encounter heavy rain that looks like heavy rain from a distance, but that keeps getting farther away as we approach it, we'll need a different kind of worry.

The perfect comfort zone now seems to be in the scariest place. It is a truly cozy area where you can wait while worrying anout a lot of things that may never happen. However, if you live in a village that will be flooded in the summer rainy season, you shouldn't worry, but you can't stop worrying. Sometimes I avoid it, but I can't feel safe if I have a family. That's what family is. Family.

I just left the door a little open, but most of the worries that the tall wind will bring everything into the room, from the yard next door to the streetside trees that sway violently in front of the house next door, get fulfilled. People we don't know will think that our wishes were fulfilled easily.

I'm standing still on the roof, but I feel as if I'm slowly going down. How shall I put it? Shall I call it a feeling of falling faster than water drops falling from the eaves? You said I was going down slowly, but that's seeing it from your viewpoint. I won't say the last drop. Because that's the water drop's business. Though it's hard for me to say it doesn't concern me.

There are not many ways of properly knowing a situation that has turned into heavy rain. It's fun talking about the weather while things are happening or after things have happened. It's a little different for people who have worried on a roof, but talking about weather is such that it truly contains a lot of lives. As well as idle worries.

You ask if I don't want to become the weather? Living and breathing is hard, but what do you think I am as I listen to your light comfort and see rice cookers floating on muddy water? Of course, I could have laughed for a few seconds when I found out that the cookers almost all were marked with the same brand. If fear takes up half of a face, something serious may happen. If fear takes up the entire face, would something worse happen? Will it be time for fear to begin to escape?

Should I move from face to face? Fears, dread, anxieties of moving from my face to your face. I do not know the crying of a mother unable to save her child. I heard it clearly, but I can't remember. I couldn't worry. Strange, but it was true. It wasn't something that saying I felt sad would solve.

Being sad and worrying are really different. Practicing losing a child must be harder than dying. But we have to do it. Since in any case we are people who have no home of our own. Because we are people who can easily lose everything. Because every time we lose something, one last chance comes back.

Don't say it's love. Only strong people can lose. Don't think that all worries are the same. Let's start a new worry. Starting with something very easy

New History

Who are you?

I ask that, taken by surprise on meeting ancient history.
It feels exactly like something I say to myself.

How many pages did the uncivilized age last?

If I turn my head more than forty-five degrees to look back while taking a walk,
the Buddha carved on a rock
seems to be stepping back into the rock

If I look for a while,

as the rock pushes the Buddha to one side

it seems to emerge.

Should I bow to the rock?

Should I bow to the Buddha?

Not knowing if it's going or coming,

I say Hello without vaguely looking at them.

The age when no one died of starvation,

the age when people who died of starvation were not buried,

the age when there were no demons,

the age when there were people more terrifying than demons,

the case of someone raving like me being executed,

the way to distinguish what happened outside

and what happened inside,

what happens when a slave goes for a walk instead of working

When countless questions turn around inside your head,

the prescription to stop thinking for once,

faced with history when you can't tell whether it's coming or going.

Autopsy

Not all memories return.
Feeling curious about the memories that couldn't return,
I became myself.

Was it in order to live?

I didn't carelessly pick up even returned memories.
It wasn't an object. Was it a true memory?
I could not be sure.

Opening myself and emerging, I was outside.
It was wide but narrow.

Little boxes were piled up.

Looking back, there was no sign of the self they had opened and come out of.

As blood oozed from my lips

I seemed to be losing myself.

Or rather, it seemed I was little by little finding as much of myself as I had lost,

Just relying on habits to live day by day,

like someone who died long ago, I

didn't breathe,

didn't eat.

The problem is I don't know what lies I'm telling.

Memories sometimes return, but when forgotten memories approached,
I didn't believe them and sent them back.

Memories sent back returned
and slashed at my hands and feet.

I didn't choose anything but
as I looked down at the flesh the memories had cut,
I wondered if I could eat that meat

And drooled.

A Museum

As there are days more precious than sunlight, as I wore a hat it's cold,
some rooms are colder than outside,
some rooms are hotter than outside,
and since there's no knowing where death is closer,
I carefully kept the cold in my body
as it's not summer now.

A reason isn't always enough, but looking back on the reason, is it too late?
How does one bid a last farewell?
The dead don't need to live worrying about every-

thing.

Sometimes, I wish I had a horse-cart, even without a horse,

And even if the sky invented by flocks of birds is full of dust

I hope I don't mistake the dust for flocks of birds, because the sky is the sky.

A dog that bit a cat and killed it is on its way to be sold tomorrow, it's sorry

but that's nothing special.

If worries can be removed from a face full of worries,
If jealousy can be eliminated from a face full of love,

Any who want to release their thoughts should raise a hand,
anyone about to gnaw their thoughts should raise a hand.

The days when people going a long way needed a map was over,
all the walls keeping off the sun were like museum

monuments.

Of course, things may smell of stories,

but that doesn't mean that everything contains stories.

One two, one two, as I can't live a single day,

do you think every day is the same? A day? If I had a day like that, it would be perfect.

As it could be recorded as the coolest lie, there'd be no need to feel ashamed,

because that's something that no one has now.

There are people who collect and objects get collected, but
finding out which object contains the most shame
is very ambiguous

Wherever you go, it will lead everywhere.
If a wall is blocking the way, you just can't cross it.
If you think a wall is joined to a wall, holding hands and blocking the way, it's still a wall, but

If you sensed someone in a house where no one lives,
maybe you love your own movements too much,

maybe it's the sorrow of getting through a day.

Bumpy Misfortune

I pay no attention to the petals that have fallen as spring passes.

Likewise, the desert where the spring vaguely gets dragged in amidst sandstorms.

Maybe it's an everyday not at all different

from the world I grew up and live in.

I couldn't catch anything, therefore

I have nothing to be resentful for.

Resentment is for some reason like the posture of one loved

squatting and crying to get love back.

As I sit by the river watching the waves
made by the ducks floating on the river,
when the biggest wave rises, I want to enter it
and calmly become the back of the surface.

Even if I can't figure out the way out.

When I cry with a wave floating in front
I can't tell you exactly that I'm the one who is crying
while scratching the back of my head

When I look down at the floor I'm sitting on
it's comforting to have a floor to look down on.

I don't know to whom it's a comfort
and to whom it's a worry
but the indifference that has to be prepared for the final calculation

That too is delicate, but if it's a bumpy indifference,
if it's an indifference out of this world

You can live unhappy repeatedly
but wishing there could be a new unhappiness is a childish kind of wish.

The Worst Habit

The cat that left the house does not come back home.

After calling its name a few times, days passed and the sun set.

The cat leaves the house and I move away from myself.

I grow older, lazier, sadder.

Even things that haven't grown grow, only I don't know.

Calling a cat's name and calling a person's name
seem to be the same but seem not to be the same.

Only then does it seem I will be human.

Sometimes people come back in containers.
They come back and soon go out again,
sometimes come back, become someone else, and go out,
become a cat and go out,
or they don't go out and don't disappear.

Even if I don't know at which scene my life stopped,
can I trust the eternal pause?

The best habit in the world is to suffer while doubting.

Do you have somewhere to go? That's what I ask myself, politely.

Hello. I give myself a greeting without return.

Hello. Stop. Switch off. Which of those words is yours?

When the person getting out of the car is me and the person waiting for the car is me,

habits open, habits close,

habits opened, habits closed

Until the worst habit gets out.

Spring Night

A small hole is drilled in winter
and through the hole
winter's guts come pouring out.
Is this spring?

I often think
I want to live a little more in this world
but that said, there is no remaining silly thought
of wanting to live like a human being leaving memories behind.

Still, a spring night is coming that will embrace me.

Tonight, while hugging the flesh inscribed with my experience
as I fully fill that flesh and spread it with the world
I walk beside a river at dawn, eager to meet the River Han
that lives by folding up the water from the Han River.

There were times when I wanted to disappear from this world every day
yet I doubt if a truly human life has ever existed in this world.

I asked for a few of the scenes I glimpsed in the Han at dawn on a spring night
as I folded up the water to be cut out and transfered to my flesh.

I don't have a heart that wants to live a human life, but
I want to live a little longer.

Walking Alone Side by Side

Darling!

Wake up.

It's a lie I'm seriously telling myself

The I who want to wake up

and live is an image

turning its back and putting out its tongue

at the I who am anxious to die.

You and I should do well.

Are the words of the dead

a sunset that the living can never hear?

Airplane tails slowly passing
above pools at sunset.

Where are you going?

The sound of soju being secretly drunk with ramen
while taking exercise walking to the Han River

This is a trajectory I can't escape from.

An obvious life
where now

it’s okay to grow no older.

Until the Han River’s waves are indistinguishable
from swollen ramen noodles

I walk side by side with myself
holding hands.

Walking Beside the River 2

I walk on because my thoughts do not go out and do not go down.

Is curbing the effort of rising with one's head a skill that must be acquired while aging?

Looking at the waves spreading after bumping into a duck half submerged in the river,

following a couple bent left and right older than me,

wondering whether or not it is the power that makes them last the day.

Whenever the waves hit the duck and spread out one after another, one small one then one large one, the waves seem to be threatening the ducks, telling them: Don't cross over; take responsibility for the waves you made; this is the last warning.

No matter how long I walk, thought does not go out, I should not, must not exaggerate and chatter that my thoughts don't go out, don't go down; stopping thoughts that don't go past is a must-do in my life.

The duck that went into the reeds does not come

out, but the riverside is ringing. I, and the couple who have hung their strength on their age, and a young man who seems to have received a duty to lose weight, walk on, not knowing that the waves they have produced have overlapped and turned into a flower.

Walking in the Sunset Foam

The sunset foam lies stretched out in the approaching evening sky.

Sunset foam boils on street corners as the sun sets and darkness comes.

Once all those bubbles disappear, night falls,

like closing one's eyes to make the dark darkness darker still.

What remains after all those bubbles have disappeared?

If I say that what remains after everything has disappeared, is the bugs that are gradually eating my life,

Even if I say that, can I catch
all those insects alive?

Was there some apology or guilt regarding life
mixed into the consolation I offered someone
while not sure why I am living?

The consolation that I felt I had to offer
although it couldn't really be considered consola-
tion,

If I think I'm living life without success
while constantly telling myself to do my job well,

I frequently think that the things I don't keep looking at are bothering me,
the things I tried to refuse to acknowledge to the bitter end
yet did or looked at are the strength enabling me to live,
if the things I can't remember
are what makes me live and embrace the world

It's a life feeling sorry for being unable to confirm it,

where nothing changes, even if I mistakenly think

I confirmed it, though

Interesting Sorrow

I knocked. A dark, interesting night. A man who went off leaving a great lesson. You say lessons flow from death? Wrapping up all at once while taking a walk. It's hard to believe, but I am a time that doesn't suit me. You just came to me and disappeared. Are you scared? So love began. No music, no alcohol, no regrets, no reluctance, no regrets to be got rid of

Just because you became an actor who briefly missed a cue doesn't mean a past appeared that you have to add to your life. At a subway station, a man is playing the guitar. Not so. The man is putting all his effort into playing himself. The mistakes were repeated. Every summer night, the I's I didn't know grew more and more numerous. Did I tell the truth?

Good ideas don't always come to mind easily. No news worth a blessing has arrived. It was a situation where anxiety close to disaster was not enough. It was an irreproachable lifetime where once was enough.

The sea is in sight. The things we long experienced and remembered in Northern European ports will become our hometown. The last lesson, that cannot be reached, cannot be stepped on. Even if I say the decisive moment in my life passed long ago, even if I say I didn't recognize it, the I who deceived me is still inside me. There is an I who will keep breathing even when I'm dead.

Although I Don't Know

A faint darkness flows past an overturned truck
and the darkness descending from the sky
and the darkness slowly starting to accumulate
make the darkness beautiful.

As the snow that fell and accumulated gradually
melts
and the darkness rises from the ground to the sky

As it rises, the darkness,
as it descends, the darkness,
as it flows, the darkness,

Becomes darkly beautiful.
As the world shuts its mouth for a moment

Will the empty wharf survive?

On the first floor there is the first floor's darkness
On the second floor there is the second floor's darkness.

At dawn, both the first and second floors turn off the lights
then the first floor's darkness and the second floor's darkness pierce the wall and hold hands

in order to grow yet darker.

On the first floor, a fruit shop owner,
on the second floor, an office worker,
on the rooftop a young man looking for a job, live

And as darkness pushed out by the moonlight and
the darkness shatter
and seep through the windows

It's hard to call them the same darkness,
it's hard to call them a different darkness.

I don't know what kind of sorrow turns into dark-
ness,
even though there is darkness in that lamplight

Spring's Temple

Take off your socks and see birds flying from under the persimmon trees and hitting the sunset

There are times when the wings of one bird are sunset. Flying into the dark as it slowly shuts its mouth

The place where I walked barefoot on temple ruins, where I walked then looked back,

not knowing that was my hometown, not knowing it's the path I have to follow, even after I die.

The ground I walked on is getting smaller. Is it the way home? I don't know if I'm looking for a place in the world where I can go crashing, breaking and unfolding. Not wondering where it is, not wasting anxiety.

Being a criminal requires more emotions. Whether it's good or bad isn't something that one person can handle. It's okay if you are someone beautiful and bad, or if you are bad but sometimes good.

Even if the happiest moments became the memories you most wanted to forget, every moment was a beautiful opportunity. But now the time to quit every opportunity is approaching.

I don't know if there are any old temples. I don't know if I'm just being broken up little by little in order to leave

With a slightly different gait.

That Is Enough

Sadness without exception

The accumulated snow is slippery

There is snow that does not disappear even when it melts

Even if it melts, there is snow that accumulates higher than the snow that accumulates

A strange life can become a meticulously built routine life that is no longer insignificant

The politeness flowing from a serious expression seems sticky to the touch

Anyone who gets angry at someone for not arriving on time is a loser

If you kindly shut your mouth and laugh, time is not so significant

Even if days and nights do not have to be grasped and got over significantly, if a broken life is repeated, nothing is the same.

There is no knowing where complex convictions come from, or why decisions continue to be put off

Is it because there is no need to rush?

Sometimes, a single voice echoes inside me. It's a sound that collapses as it rises, so I don't know what it's saying.

If we attract worries, does that mean entering into the worries? Or getting out of the worries?

Are you worried that if something dries, it cannot

be erased, and remains after erasing?

This house is poorly designed. Still, people can live and people can die inside it

Maybe so long as we are alive, total failure is impossible. Is that a kind of luck?

I want to say hello when I see a fireplace. It's a neat and attractive tragedy. I feel a painful happiness

It doesn't matter if you have great difficulty in living

Fights that cannot be won are always important. But may I fight in order to lose?

I'm looking at you because it's difficult for me to look at me. That is enough

One Evening's Snow

Will I be able to reach myself?

Still alive

if I can just touch it once

I think I can live my life again.

In order to reach myself,

close but not able to reach myself,

how many people should I meet

among the people I should meet?

Even if I reckon it can't be helped

since I have already overflowed or flowed away.

Snow is falling.

Not much.

just a little

The snow that is falling

does not accumulate and does not melt.

Order

Tears increased after you left.

After you left I spent my life floundering in tears.

And now

there is almost nothing left to call "I".

From the moment you left

I've been becoming you.

Isn't every struggle in the world to get out of the world

love?

Traces of striving to embrace more tightly,
even if it hurts

Tears increased a great deal after you left.
If I go out to the riverside and count the waves one by one
night falls, but

Tears now overtake me and live this life,
so I'm curious about what number man I am.

I'm curious what number empty man I am.

Early Spring

Spring has still come less. It's not even a courier
Into a life without time to think of the rest of spring
spring has come less.

Holding a spoon and looking for a spoon
when I look at the rice piled in a bowl blankly
the weight of the spoon held in my hand is transmitted to the wrist.

Am I used to living deceived by thoughts?

Thinking like moss, a mane of green moss,

the limitations necessary for life while shaking

If there's still any left, I want to borrow it.

Bridal-wreath trees and fringe trees are not similar at all,
and now to distinguish between the two trees
I have to meet people or search in books,
But in this life, I repeatedly forget
and I'm happy to have a name I can repeatedly regain.

No one knows, I don't use this word anymore.

The sadness I thought I owned,
wasn't mine and yet
it also wasn't a legacy that someone had left behind

If you keep claiming to the bitter end that it's mine,
I don't know if it's an illusion and freedom to enjoy in this life to the end

Snow falls
I want to melt and freeze there like an expectation.

POET'S NOTES

I like going for walks. I especially like walking very slowly beside a river. I walk more slowly than the river and look at the people passing me. Some people I see every day because the time when I take a walk is constant. Even if we meet each other at the same time or at a similar place, we do not greet each other, but today we feel safe. I don't ask how they feel, but I hope that the people I met yesterday and those I am making this walk with today, will continue.

There is no way to let go of worries. That's why I often think that I should do what I worry about together. Both small worries and big worries are essential for living. It is one of the must-dos if you are alive. The question is anxiety about how to share these big and small worries. It's okay if you don't approach each other at first. There are many ways you can worry about each other without sharing voices or shaking hands.

There is no same time, same place in this world. Once it passes, everything is new, so your worries should be refreshed. Yesterday's worries do not have to be resolved today or tomorrow. Sometimes, sharing your worries with someone will be more important than addressing them. While walking, I bumped into someone for a while and we greeted each other. It feels like we have exchanged worries about each other, although we have done nothing more than just nodding at each other, or sharing a glance.

Poetry may be a matter of increasing your worries by staying with your daily life. At first, my worries are more important than anything else in the world, but when the moment comes when the worries of others feel like mine, the small worries are changed into ethical clothes. However, just as I did yesterday, today too I would like to share my worries for a long time, just as I live my daily life without being bombastic.

POET'S ESSAY

Memory

There is no way to escape from memory. People who can keep good memories for a long time are happy people. However, people who can keep bad memories for a long time are also happy people. Because they are alive. Even without evoking religion, humans must live in pain. Also, there are countless things to overcome from moment to moment. Of course, the record of numerous failures is what I am now, and I have to live with more failures in the future. Many people think that small successes are what make their lives worth living, but they don't realize that 'being alive' goes beyond successes and failures in enabling them to live this life.

I don't remember my sadness very well. This is because there are many cases where, on looking back after feeling sad, it turns out to be nothing. But I remember your sadness well. Your sadness is clear and hard to erase, even though you have never asked me to recognize your grief, to remember it, or to comfort you. I don't know if it's because I'm empty inside that I easily forget about myself. But I can't forget about you because you become more and more distinct as you fill the emptiness within me. My sorrow is also precious, but when I come to know of your sorrow, my sorrow starts to disappear as if it had never existed.

It's raining. A cat walks under the eaves to avoid the rain. As it walks, it looks back and cries. After a while, two baby cats come under the eaves and are embraced by the mother cat, guarding them in all directions. There are many ways to avoid the rain, but the way to avoid the rain when alone and the way to avoid the rain when in a group seems to be very different. What many need to avoid the rain is love. It's small so it's invisible, and it's so small that you can't notice the feeling even though someone has begun to love. That is love. Most of the time, love passes by. So wait until you notice that love.

One day, three cats that have come to our house are taking a nap. Two baby cats are growing differently every day, and my mother feeds them every day. The cat that first came every few days has now become the master of our house. Of course, its masters are all three cats. Two baby cats and one mother cat. It seems that they only eat food and are not interested in humans. My mother is getting so old. The three cats are napping in the yard and Mother napping on the sofa. Sometimes we think about how firmly the 'eaves of sleep' protect us. Anyway, my house has been taken over by three cats, and my mother and I have become the cats' butlers.

The world has become noisy with the corona virus. It is because our daily life is cracked. Meeting people is becoming more important. Even if it wasn't a special meeting, going to the cinema, going to the market, and going on a trip had become very important. It seems that I have come to realize how valuable things are that I have never considered precious. Of course, the daily life changed by the corona is also important. Long stays in private spaces, non-face-to-face classes, people drinking tea from a distance, etc. Even if not for a very long time, daily life due to the virus will also remain a valuable experience along with daily life before the coronavirus.

The books I had deposited in a warehouse were

soaked in water. The roof of the warehouse was torn off by the wind and rain poured out. I received one book soaked by the rain. It may be a book I cannot turn a single page, or it may be a book with only one page. A book that will long remain in my memory emerged. A book that I couldn't read emerged.

It was afternoon. There was no fog, but it was a summer that felt like fog. Our three-year-old daughter was walking home from far away. My wife followed her. It was late on a Saturday afternoon. It was the day I met my daughter and wife a few months after finishing work at the factory. Our daughter came walking from far away. I lifted up my daughter to hug her, but my daughter hugged me. Tears flowed. I didn't know why. It seemed to be something that I could never know in my lifetime. It's been fifteen years. Sometimes I go back to fifteen years ago, go back and ask why I cried. But the

I of fifteen years ago is silent.

At 5 am, the first train passes near our house. Our house, being close to the railroad tracks, shakes. The walls shake and the floor shakes. Sometimes I wake up. Sometimes I am surprised. Is it because the train makes me sway so that I wake up in surprise and in fear? The train does not pass only at 5 am. At other times they pass about once an hour. The 5 a.m. train has become an object of fear. I am surprised even when I am awake, and wake up in amazement even when I am sleeping. The 5 am train is fear. After a while, it will be 5 am. However, it is not something fixed, so that it is always 5 am.

I wasted a lot of energy trying to escape from memory. I loved going on journeys because I didn't want to remember bad memories. When I met something new, I needed tension. When I was nervous, a lot of concentration was required at that moment. I was able to forget things that had happened long ago. I often travelled, not realizing that forgetting doesn't mean disappearing. When I came back from a trip, I had bad memories returned again. While leaving again and again and again, I was missing many things. I had to live in the world while accepting bad memories, but I wanted only good things. I was stupid.

COMMENTARY

To the poet who lives by the railroad

Kim Do-yeon (novelist)

I have the impression that I paid a visit to your remote country house in the middle of the night. It was midnight and a faint light came seeping out of the house, as we stood at the entrance of the house exchanging a few words. I seem to have asked you about the train tracks located like a fortress next door. Wasn't the sound of the passing trains loud? You seem to have answered neither positively nor negatively in your characteristic slow tones. Perhaps you said that the sound of high-speed trains, ordinary trains, and freight trains was different... That night we came back without entering the house where you live. As we returned, I kept thinking of you lying face downward in your small room next to the railroad tracks slowly coaxing out poems matching your frame. A poet surprised from time to time by the sound of a train. I never once thought of a dung beetle making and rolling rice balls.

The first time I saw you was at the home of Professor Shim, who studied Indian philosophy. It had been a long time since your debut, but you had not yet published a collection of poems. Starting like that, we met at this bar or that bar in Wonju and emptied glasses. I've mentioned drinking, but I didn't really like your foolishly elevated drinking habits. One day, we were kicked out of a bar in Gangneung while we were drinking. But you were different. One day, I got drunk at a funeral wake in Seoul and you brought me back to Wonju, as I rolled along like a table tennis ball. I have nothing to say. Anyway, in the meantime, you lay in your small house next to the train tracks turning the pages of your first and second collections of poetry. This is a night when I want to say thank you again.

This relationship led me to write the epilogue for your third poetry book, but in fact it was very difficult. How much did I know about poetry as a novelist? I just liked poetry back then. So the method I chose was to just read your poems one by one. While reading, I decided to sit down for a moment and look at the sky where clouds were floating.

> Holding a spoon and looking for a spoon / when I look at the rice piled in a bowl blankly / the weight of the spoon held in my hand is transmitted to the wrist. // Bridal-wreath trees and fringe trees are not similar at all, / and now to distinguish between the two trees / I have to meet people or search in books, / But in

this life, I repeatedly forget / and I'm happy to have a name I can repeatedly regain. (Early Spring)

Tears now overtake me and live this life, / so I'm curious about what number man I am. // I'm curious what number empty man I am. (Order)

This house is poorly designed. Still, people can live and people can die inside it // Maybe so long as we are alive, total failure is impossible. Is that a kind of luck? (That Is Enough)

Names so similar that I forgot them. I picture the face of an empty, shabby man who is looking for a spoon that seems to have been lost, so used to it he has become. Yes, like you said, what number man are we? What kind of life will the tears that have overtaken us live? I bow my head, admitting a failed life, but you nod and call it luck.

Even if the happiest moments became the memories you most wanted to forget, every moment was a beautiful opportunity. But now the time to quit every opportunity is approaching. (Spring's Temple)

On the first floor there is the first floor's darkness / On the second floor there is the second floor's darkness. // It's hard to call them the same darkness, / it's hard to call them a different darkness. (Although I Don't Know)

Just because you became an actor who briefly missed a cue doesn't mean a past appeared that you have to add to your life. At a subway station, a man is playing the guitar. Not so. The man is putting all his effort into playing himself. The mistakes were repeated. Every summer night, the I's I didn't know grew more and more numerous. Did I tell the truth? (Interesting Sorrow)

Was there some apology or guilt regarding life / mixed into the consolation I offered someone / while not sure why I am living? (Walking in the Sunset Foam)

Joo-cheol, it turns out that we took the same train twice. Once you were drunk and another time I was drunk. One was the night train from Seoul to Wonju and the other was a day train from Wonju to Gangneung. You snooped under the seats where other people were sitting in search of the ping pong balls I was spilling, saying that I kept spilling very small and light ping pong balls. Sorry and thank you. On the train to Gangneung, I didn't even know you were so drunk, so how could I have comforted your sadness? I'm sorry. Who were we really at that time? That darkness and brightness were light shining on what person on which floor? What did I say to you then?

No matter how long I walk, thought does not go out,
I should not, must not exaggerate and chatter that

my thoughts don't go out, don't go down; stopping thoughts that don't go past is a must-do in my life. (Walking Beside the River 2)

Still, a spring night is coming that will embrace me. (Spring Night)

The best habit in the world is to suffer while doubting. (The Worst Habit)

Resentment is for some reason like the posture of one loved / squatting and crying to get love back. (Bumpy Misfortune)

If you sensed someone in a house where no one lives, / maybe you love your own movements too much, / maybe it's the sorrow of getting through a day. (A Museum)

In the meantime, Joo-cheol, something happened. I didn't see you for a while, but I just thought you would be fine in your room next to the train track. I'm sorry, but I must admit that I know very little about you. I don't feel comfortable because I don't know anything about your sadness, so I feel like I've been giving a lot of poor advice. Even if I couldn't go to a bar because of the world of Corona, I could still sit on the bank of the Dangang River with a bottle of soju and get drunk watching the sunset. Still, I'm glad there was a spring night that hugged you.

Memories sometimes return, but when forgotten memories approached, / I didn't believe them and sent them back. (Autopsy)

Not knowing if it's going or coming, / I say Hello without vaguely looking at them. (New History)

I just left the door a little open, but most of the worries that the tall wind will bring everything into the room, from the yard next door to the streetside trees that sway violently in front of the house next door, get fulfilled. People we don't know will think that our wishes were fulfilled easily. (Let's Start Worrying)

> Why don't unconfirmed feelings stop? (Feeling Does Not Stop)
>
> The snack bar kid approaches perfection while dictating, / dumpling soup when the dumplings are cooked and float, / noodles when they approach the broth that enables them to recall memories, / chairs when they are repeatedly filled with hips. // They approach completion, but are not complete. (The Completed Snack Bar)

Oh, Joo-cheol. There was a time when you were talking about poetry in a library in Wonju. At that time, you invited Professor Shim and me for an uninteresting drinking party and did not invite us for a very interesting drinking party. Of course, it was only your choice, but Professor Shim and I were very disappointed looking at the photos of that day. Professor Shim raised his voice, saying, 'That XX Joo-cheol has excluded us and is having fun on his own.' Joo-cheol, we can't all be perfect, but shouldn't we try to get close to it like in your poems? In fact, Professor Shim and I are lonely people when you get to know us.

In order to use the remaining strength, I walk beside the river // Taking the dog, / having gone out taking the dog dragging myself along hard (Walking Beside the River 1)

that does not become sorrow, / does not form an edge for tears. (Informal Sorrow)

I cannot get to sleep / because I live with the things I fear / or maybe because I secretly enjoy them. (Turning Off the Light and Lying Down)

Darkness was entering / through that back. (Someone with an Open Back)

As I said earlier, Joo-cheol, I am a person who is not familiar with poetry. As I read your poems, I have only a slight ability to glimpse your thoughts. All I can do is tilt my head or nod while looking at the titles of your poems several times.

You muttered quietly that you wanted to share worries with your neighbors and that you wanted to remember your neighbor's sadness better than your own. You also complained that it was foolish to waste so much energy trying to escape from memory. You confessed that you had to live in the world while accepting bad memories, but wanted only good things. Yes, that is clearly the way of human beings, but we feel embarrassed as it seems that we have become monsters devoted only to our own worries and sadness.

I enjoyed reading the poems. It's a night when the three of us long to sit in your small room by the railroad and drink while listening to the sound of trains passing by.

WHAT THEY SAY ABOUT AHN JOO-CHEOL

K POET

When we read Ahn Joo-cheol's poems, we think of evening. At the time when the sun goes down, objects receive the glow of sunset and extend their shadows. It's time for them to let loose the darkness they had been harboring. Just as the sun, having risen, finally passes beyond the western hills, everything that comes into the world will ultimately encounter its own evening. Living also involves disappearing. As they disappear thus, things that exist also accumulate in themselves as much darkness as they have lived, secrets that cannot be revealed.

Tae-seon Kim, 「Exploration of Flowers」(Commentary on: "I'm Only Alive When I'm Anxious") Munhakdongne, 2020

K-POET
Feeling Never Stops

Written by Ahn Joo-cheol | **Translated by** Brother Anthony of Taizè
Published by ASIA Publishers | 445, Hoedong-gil, Paju-si, Gyeonggi-do, Korea
(Seoul Office: 161-1, Seodal-ro, Dongjak-gu, Seoul, Korea)
Homepage Address www.bookasia.org | **Tel** (822).821.5055 | **Fax** (822).821.5057
ISBN 979-11-5662-317-5 (set) | 979-11-5662-515-5 (04810)
First published in Korea by ASIA Publishers 2020

This book is published with the support of the Literature Translation Institute of Korea(LTI Korea).

K-픽션 한국 젊은 소설

최근에 발표된 단편소설 중 가장 우수하고 흥미로운 작품을 엄선하여 출간하는 〈K-픽션〉은 한국문학의 생생한 현장을 국내외 독자들과 실시간으로 공유하고자 기획되었습니다. 원작의 재미와 품격을 최대한 살린 〈K-픽션〉 시리즈는 매 계절마다 새로운 작품을 선보입니다.

001 버핏과의 저녁 식사-**박민규** Dinner with Buffett-**Park Min-gyu**

002 아르판-**박형서** Arpan-**Park hyoung su**

003 애드벌룬-**손보미** Hot Air Balloon-**Son Bo-mi**

004 나의 클린트 이스트우드-**오한기** My Clint Eastwood-**Oh Han-ki**

005 이베리아의 전갈-**최민우** Dishonored-**Choi Min-woo**

006 양의 미래-**황정은** Kong' s Garden-**Hwang Jung-eun**

007 대니-**윤이형** Danny-**Yun I-hyeong**

008 퇴근-**천명관** Homecoming-**Cheon Myeong-kwan**

009 옥화-**금희** Ok-hwa-**Geum Hee**

010 시차-**백수린** Time Difference-**Baik Sou linne**

011 올드 맨 리버-**이장욱** Old Man River-**Lee Jang-wook**

012 권순찬과 착한 사람들-**이기호** Kwon Sun-chan and Nice People-**Lee Ki-ho**

013 알바생 자르기-**장강명** Fired-**Chang Kangmyoung**

014 어디로 가고 싶으신가요-**김애란** Where Would You Like To Go?-**Kim Ae-ran**

015 세상에서 가장 비싼 소설-**김민정** The World' s Most Expensive Novel-**Kim Min-jung**

016 체스의 모든 것-**김금희** Everything About Chess-**Kim Keum-hee**

017 할로윈-**정한아** Halloween-**Chung Han-ah**

018 그 여름-**최은영** The Summer-**Choi Eunyoung**

019 어느 피씨주의자의 종생기-**구병모** The Story of P.C.-**Gu Byeong-mo**

020 모르는 영역-**권여선** An Unknown Realm-**Kwon Yeo-sun**

021 4월의 눈-**손원평** April Snow-**Sohn Won-pyung**

022 서우-**강화길** Seo-u-**Kang Hwa-gil**

023 가출-**조남주** Run Away-**Cho Nam-joo**

024 연애의 감정학-**백영옥** How to Break Up Like a Winner-**Baek Young-ok**

025 창모-**우다영** Chang-mo-**Woo Da-young**

026 검은 방-**정지아** The Black Room-**Jeong Ji-a**

027 도쿄의 마야-**장류진** Maya in Tokyo-**Jang Ryu-jin**

can meet the real Korea!

Korean Literature

22 keywords to understand Korean literature

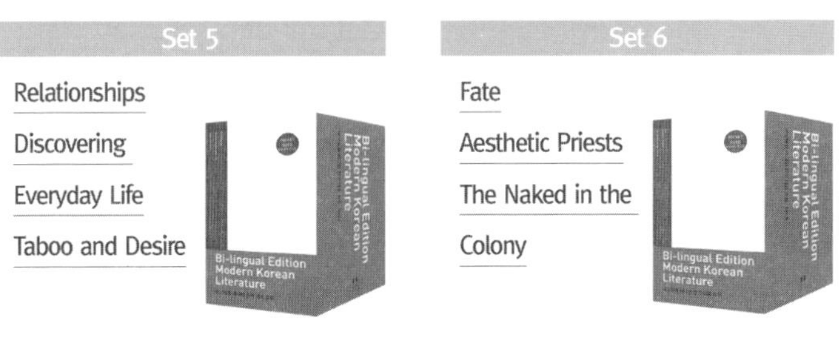

Set 7

Colonial Intellectuals Turned “Idiots”

Traditional Korea’s Lost Faces

Before and After Liberation

Korea After the Korean War

korean literature”on Amazon!